TIM JEFFS ART
Animal Sketches
ENDANGERED
Baby
ANIMALS
VOLUME 2

A Special Edition Coloring Book

For Jane, Jenna and Harrison

Dedicated to all of the wonderful colorists who have supported my art and made my drawings more beautiful with their colors, and all the precious creatures that we live among.
A special thank you to Jo Warren for all of her continued support and beautiful colorings and lesson that make this book so much more special, and Karl Jennings for all of his continued support.

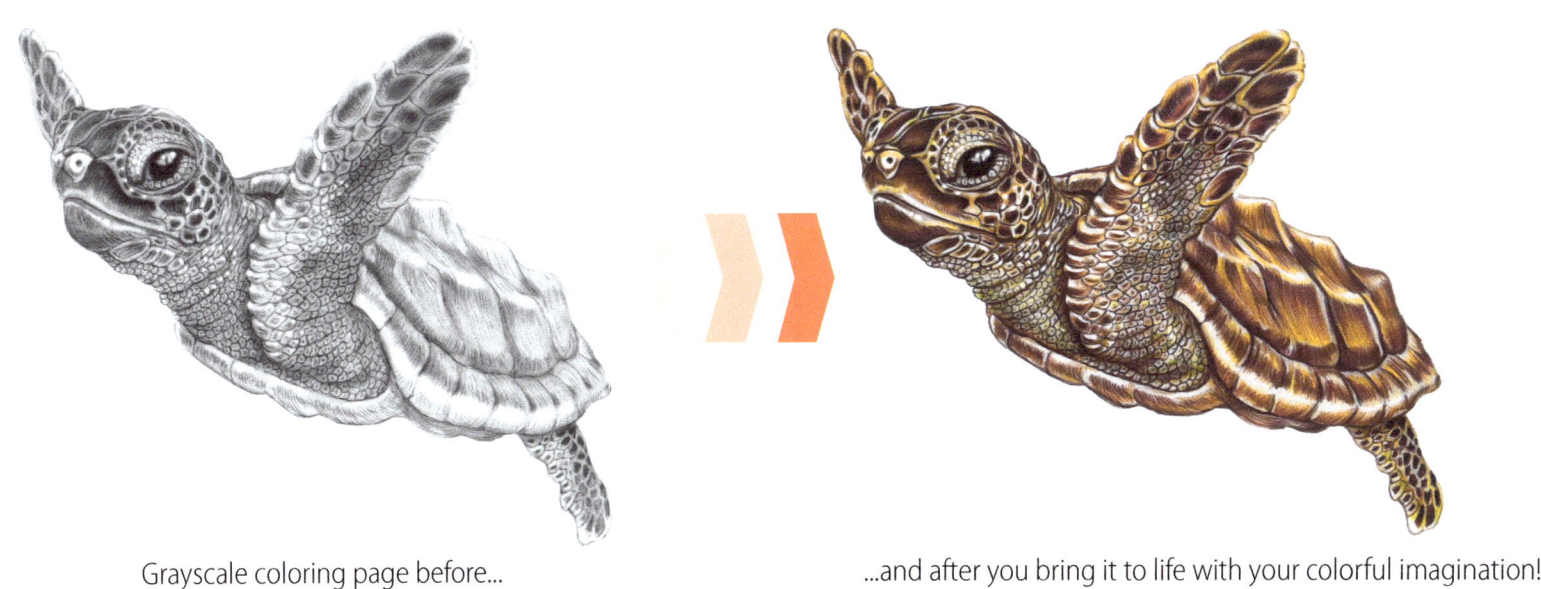

Grayscale coloring page before...   ...and after you bring it to life with your colorful imagination!

© Copyright 2022 Tim Jeffs Art
All rights reserved. No part of this publication may be reproduced or
distributed in any form without the prior written permission of Tim Jeffs Art.

Tim Jeffs Art
376 East Madison Avenue, Dumont, NJ 07628

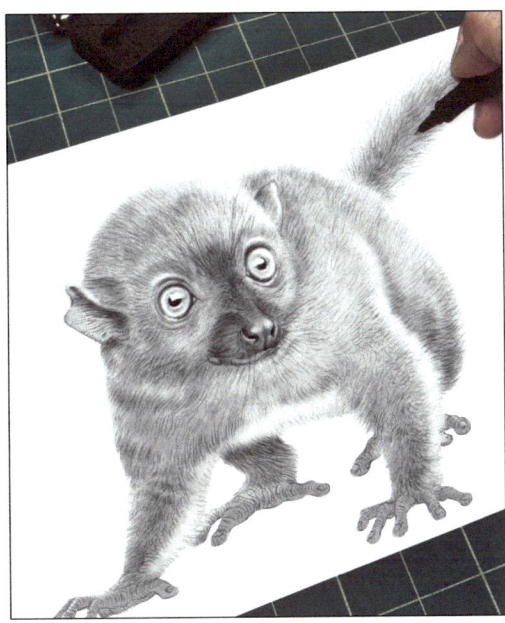 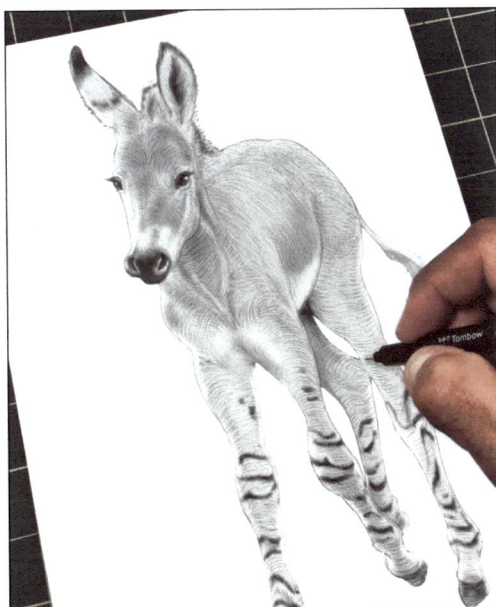 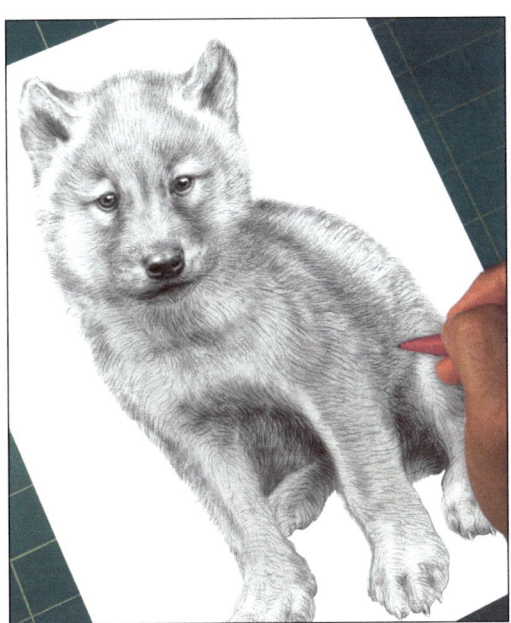

Endangered Baby Animal Sketches Thoughts

The Baby Animals Are Back! They tug on our hearts, they make us smile, and give us hope that the next generation of their species will thrive. After the wonderful response to my first endangered baby animals coloring book I want to continue to bring awareness to even more threatened animals. So many animals deserve a fighting chance to live in peace in their wild habitats, and these babies are the true fighters that will make it a reality.

I'm so happy to be able to continue to give colorists what they love, more baby animal drawings to color. And even more importantly a coloring book that will help raise awareness of endangered animals as it's being enjoyed. My hope is while you color these precious baby animals you realize that the animals that are struggling to survive need our utmost attention. Coloring and sharing your creative work from this book is a wonderful way to make a difference.

I hope you enjoy coloring this group of endangered baby animal sketches as much as I enjoyed drawing them, and I know that with your colors, you will bring them running, playing, and climbing to life! Have fun!

GRAYSCALE COLORING LESSON
Sea Otters

Lesson level: *Easy*

Coloring a
Mother Sea Otter And Her Pup

❱ Supply List

In this lesson, Fc Polychromos pencils were used, (pencil numbers listed below) but you can use any brand with similar colors.

1) **The coloring page can be found on page 13**

2) **Colors:** (103) Ivory • (175) Dark Sepia • (180) Raw Umber • (199) Black • (283) Burnt Sienna

3) **Pencil Sharpener:** An electric pencil sharpener is easy to use and works best to keep your pencils extra sharp and your hand less sore. But if you don't have one, no problem. A hand pencil sharpener works just fine too.

On the next page I will walk you through the coloring of the Sea Otter mother and her adorable pup which you can find on page 13 of this coloring book. Coloring fur can be very easy if you know a few tips to achieve a fluffy and soft look. Once you have learned these easy steps you can apply them in all your future furry colorings. When you are finished remember to share your coloring of these super cute animals and help spread awareness of their endangered status.

GRAYSCALE COLORING LESSON
Sea Otters

Sea Otter Mother and Her Pup Coloring Lesson

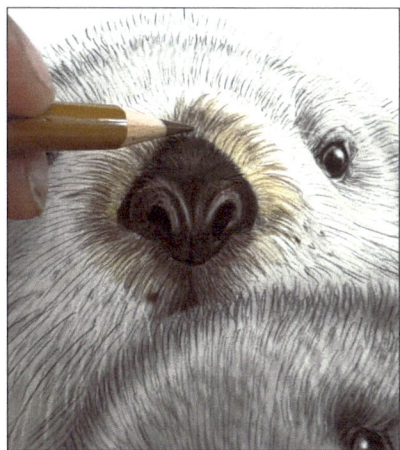

Step 1. Color the mother's and babies otters nose using (175) Dark Sepia. Leave the area above each nostril lighter. Working from the nose outward color fine lines using (180) Raw Umber.

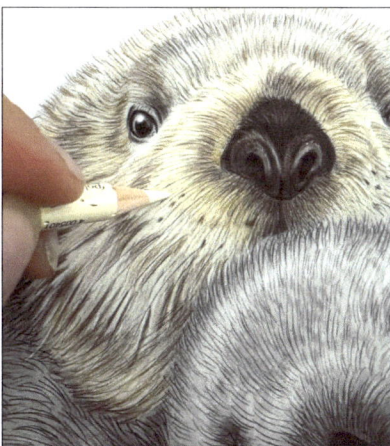

Step 2. One trick to creating soft and fluffy fur is to layer lighter colors over darker ones. Using (103) Ivory blend strokes over top of the Raw Umber lines. Continue this layering across the entire head.

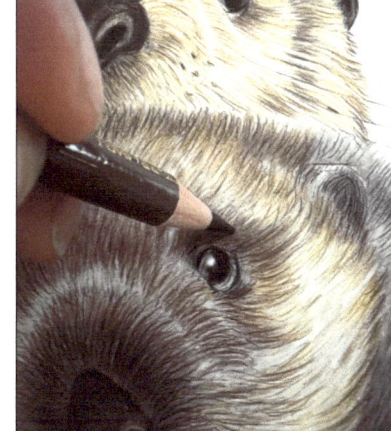

Step 3. The baby otter will be darker than the mother otter. Using (175) Dark Sepia color strokes following the lines in the drawing. Then blend a layer of lighter brown over the top using (283) Burnt Sienna. Color (103) Ivory on lightest areas of the face.

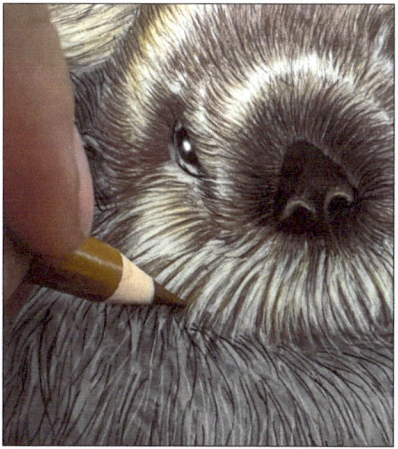

Step 4. To achieve the bristly look of the baby otter's whiskers color the dark areas between each whisker using (180) Raw Umber, and then color each whisker with (103) Ivory. The more you build up these colors the more the whiskers will appear individual.

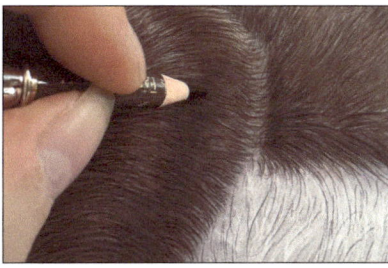
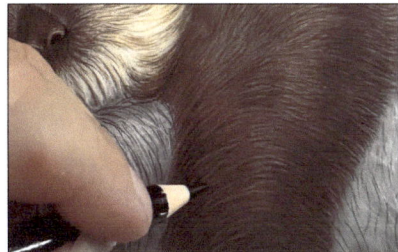

Step 5. The Baby otters fur should be very dark, so the more you build up color the better. Using fine short strokes layer (175) Dark Sepia and (283) Burnt Sienna. Finally to create shape color (199) Black around the outer edges of the pups arm, belly, and back.

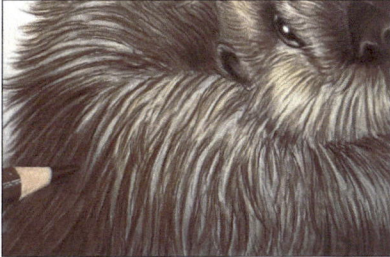
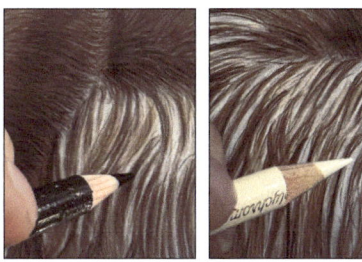

Step 6. To contrast the mother's body against the baby otter's dense fur color her fur with thicker and longer looking hairs. Do this by increasing the length of each stroke as you color. Alternate between dark, medium, and light hairs. Use (103) Ivory to add highlights.

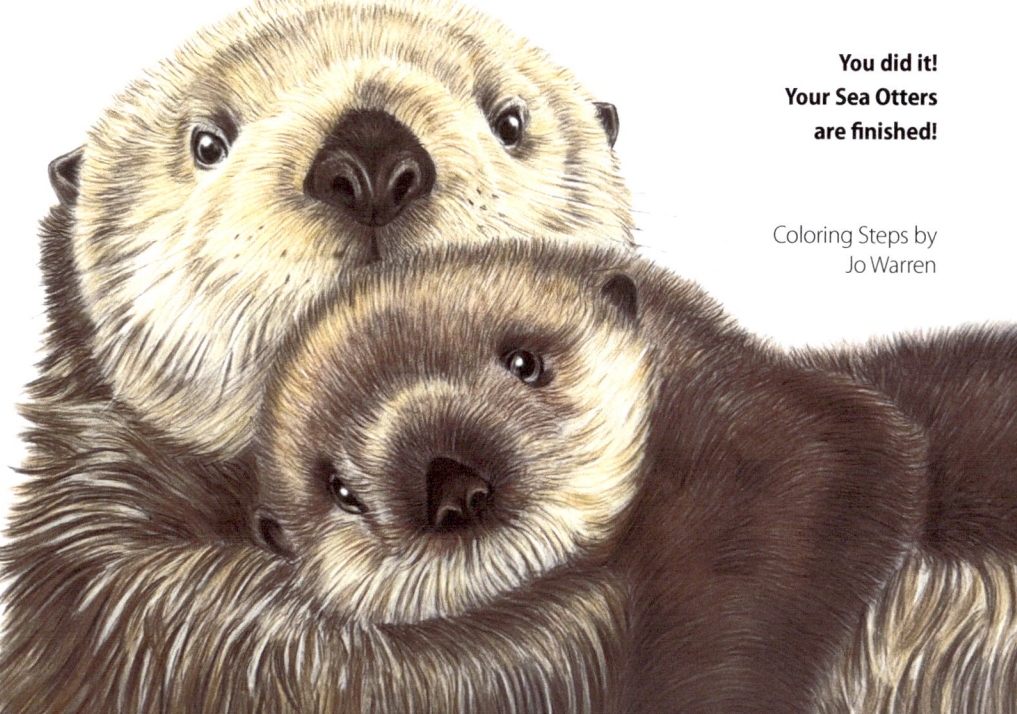

**You did it!
Your Sea Otters
are finished!**

Coloring Steps by
Jo Warren

Spreading Awareness through Coloring

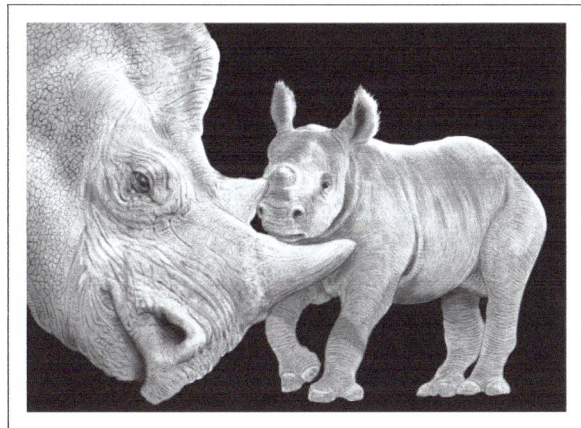

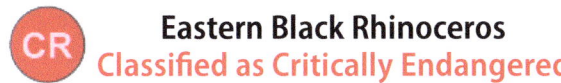

Eastern Black Rhinoceros
Classified as Critically Endangered

I truly believe that raising awareness through the sharing of my artwork is a fantastic way to educate people about conservation. And coloring animals is a beautiful way to learn about them as you enjoy a relaxing and fun pastime. On the following page, I listed the baby animals statuses on the *International Union for Conservation of Nature's (IUCN)* conservation list. I think it's important to include the *(IUCN)* conservation list so people understand the classifications more clearly. To the right is an overview of the IUCN's conservation list, which breaks animals' conservation statuses into several categories. Knowing what these categories mean and the animals that are included in them is extremely important. **Together through art and coloring we can change the world!**

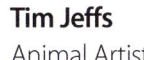

Tim Jeffs
Animal Artist

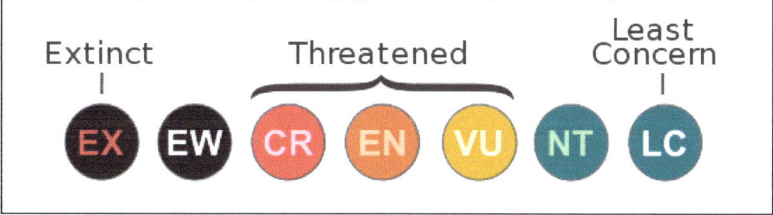

The list consists of 7 categories. From Least Concerned all the way to Extinct. Here are the definitions of each category:

- **LEAST CONCERN (LC):** A species that has been evaluated but not qualified for any other category on the list.
- **NEAR THREATENED (NT):** A species that may be considered threatened with extinction in the near future.
- **VULNERABLE (VU):** A species likely to become endangered unless the circumstances that are threatening its survival and reproduction improve.
- **ENDANGERED (EN):** A species that is considered very likely to become extinct.
- **CRITICALLY ENDANGERED (CR):** A species that is facing an extremely high risk of becoming extinct in the wild.
- **EXTINCT IN THE WILD (EW):** A species that is only known by living members kept in captivity or as a naturalized population outside its historic range due to massive habitat loss.
- **EXTINCT (EX):** A species that has been terminated.

Learn about the Endangered Baby Animals

Before you start coloring, it's important to learn why the baby animals in this book are considered endangered and how important conservation efforts are to save these animals.

❱ African Forest Elephant
Due to habitat loss and poaching for ivory their population has decreased by more than 80% over 3 generations. 415,000 left in the wild.
Conservation Status: Critically Endangered

❱ Blue-Eyed Black Lemur
Most of their habitat has been clear cut for farmland making it nearly extinct in the wild. As few as 1,000 individuals remain in the wild.
Conservation Status: Critically Endangered

❱ Cotton-Top Tamarins
6,000 individuals remain in the wild. The main reason for their decline is habitat destruction through forest clearing.
Conservation Status: Critically Endangered

❱ Eastern Black Rhinoceros
Illegal poaching for their horn has been the main cause of their decline. Only 470 individuals are estimated to live in the wild.
Conservation Status: Critically Endangered

❱ Great Green Macaw
Due to habitat loss, in Costa Rica it is considered at risk of extinction. The world population is estimated at 1,000 to 2,500 birds.
Conservation Status: Critically Endangered

❱ Hawksbill Sea Turtle
Their population has declined 80% in the last 100 years. Major threats are pollution and loss of nesting areas. Worldwide there are only 1,000 females nesting annually.
Conservation Status: Critically Endangered

❱ Mhorr Gazelle
Less then 500 individuals live in the wild and little has been done to help save them due to little to no action being done from the poor countries which they occur in.
Conservation Status: Critically Endangered

❱ Mountain Bongo
Threatened by illegal hunting there are less than 100 wild Mountain Bongo's left in Central Africa today.
Conservation Status: Critically Endangered

❱ Pangolin
Threatened by misinformation that their scales have medicinal properties, their meat is considered a delicacy, and the destruction of their habitat Pangolin numbers have suffered greatly.
Conservation Status: Endangered

❱ Pygmy Hippopotamus
Like so many other animals loss of habitat has been their biggest threat. The forests where they live are subject to logging. 2000-3000 remain in the wild.
Conservation Status: Endangered

❱ Red Wolf
Only an estimated 35 or fewer Red Wolves live in the wild. They are isolated to a small area in Southeast Texas while their range used to be most of the Southern and Eastern United States.
Conservation Status: Critically Endangered

❱ Scottish Wildcat
Inbreeding with domestic cats, habitat loss and being hunted as vermin there are estimated to be fewer than 100 existing in the wild.
Conservation Status: Critically Endangered

❱ Sea Otter
Hunted extensively for their fur from the 1700s-1900s their numbers dropped from 300,000 to as few as 1,000. A ban on hunting has helped their numbers rebound to an estimated 16,000.
Conservation Status: Endangered

❱ Snow Leopard
Listed by the IUCN as endangered since 1986 the Snow Leopard's status has been recently downgraded to vulnerable. Though still in decline and in need of urgent conservation measures, I wanted to include one success story in this group of animals.
Conservation Status: Vulnerable

❱ Somalia Wild Ass
With less than 1000 animals in the wild this species faces a high risk of extinction in the wild. Breeding programs are increasing their numbers.
Conservation Status: Critically Endangered

Endangered Baby Animals Index

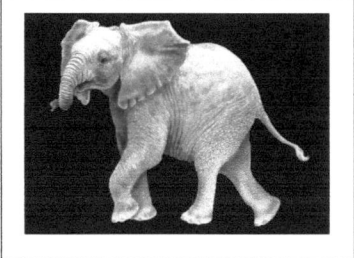
African Forest Elephant 1

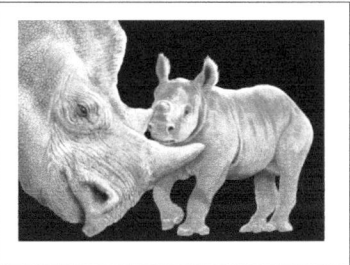
Eastern Black Rhinoceros 4

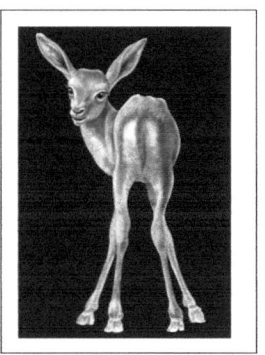
Mhorr Gazelle 7

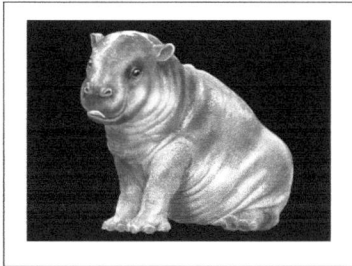
Pygmy Hippopotamus 10

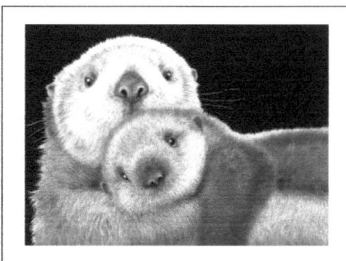
Sea Otters 13

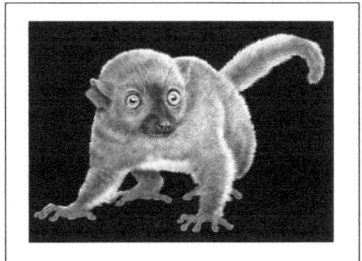
Blue-Eyed Black Lemur 2

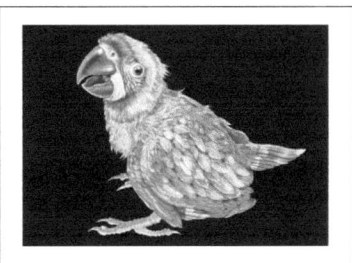
Great Green Macaw 5

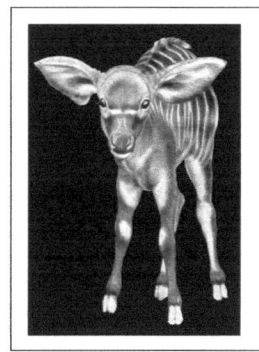
Mountain Bongo 8

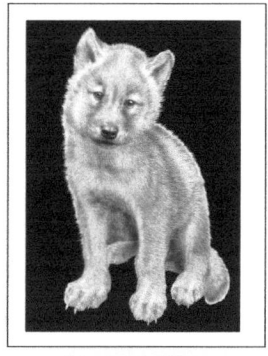
Red Wolf 11

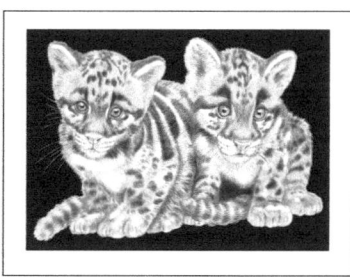
Snow Leopards 14

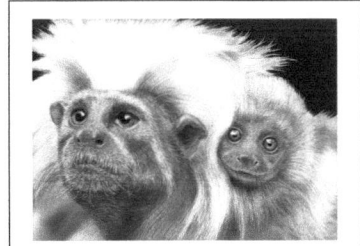
Cotton-Top Tamarins 3

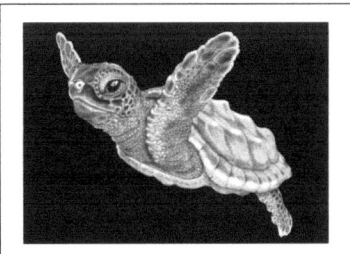
Hawksbill Sea Turtle 6

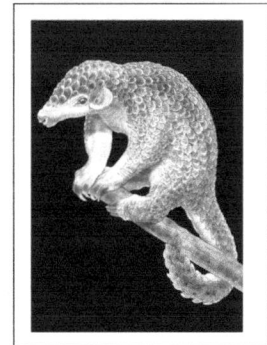
Pangolin 9

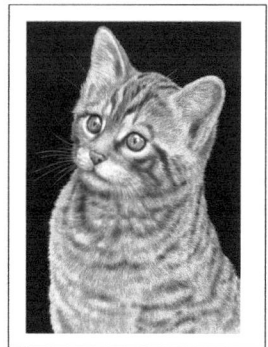
Scottish Wildcat 12

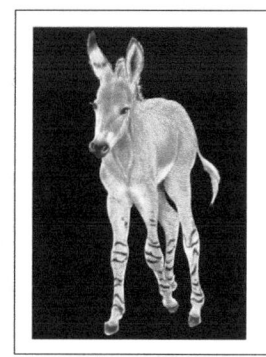
Somalia Wlld Ass 15

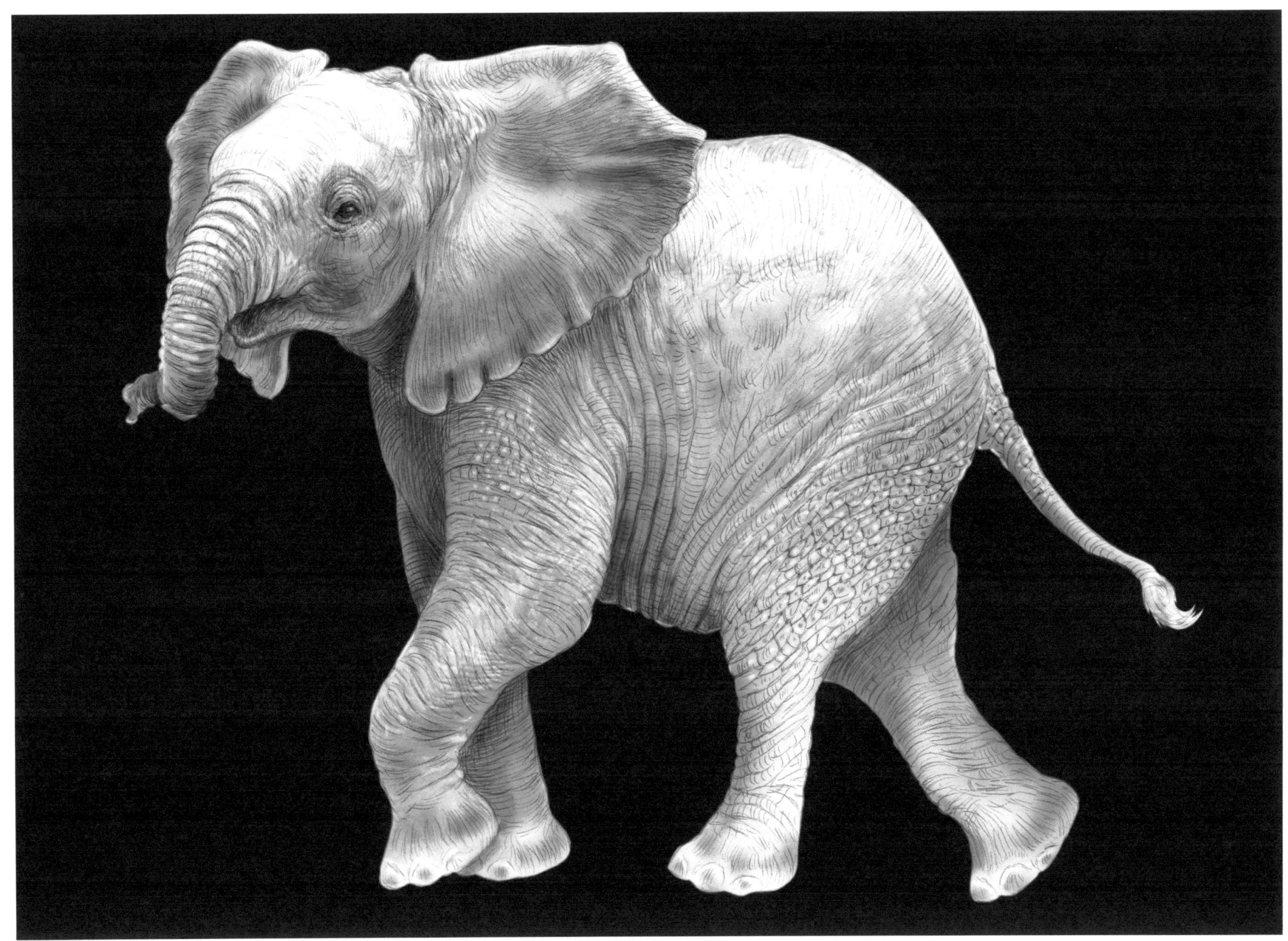

African Forest Elephant

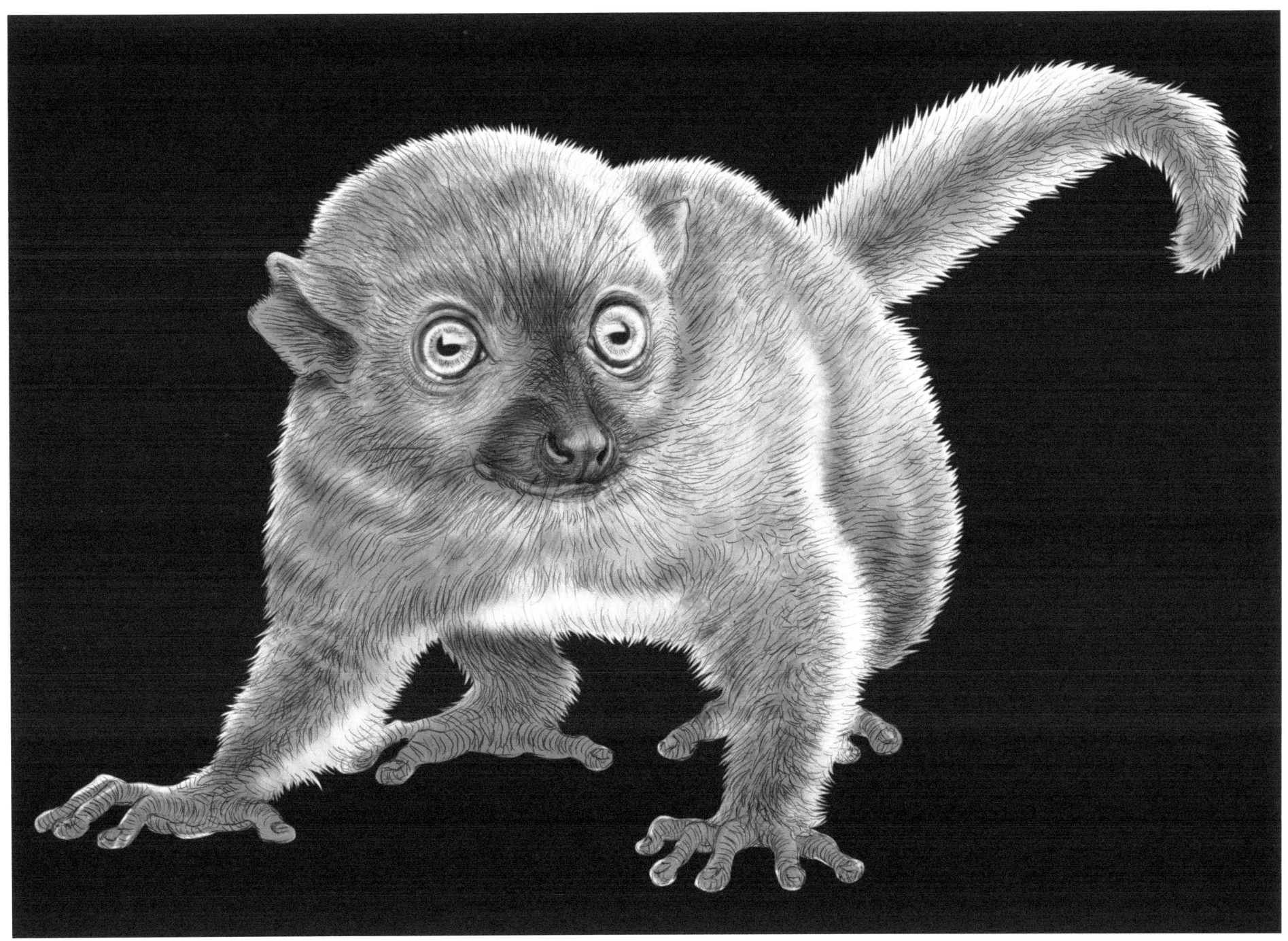

Blue-Eyed Black Lemur

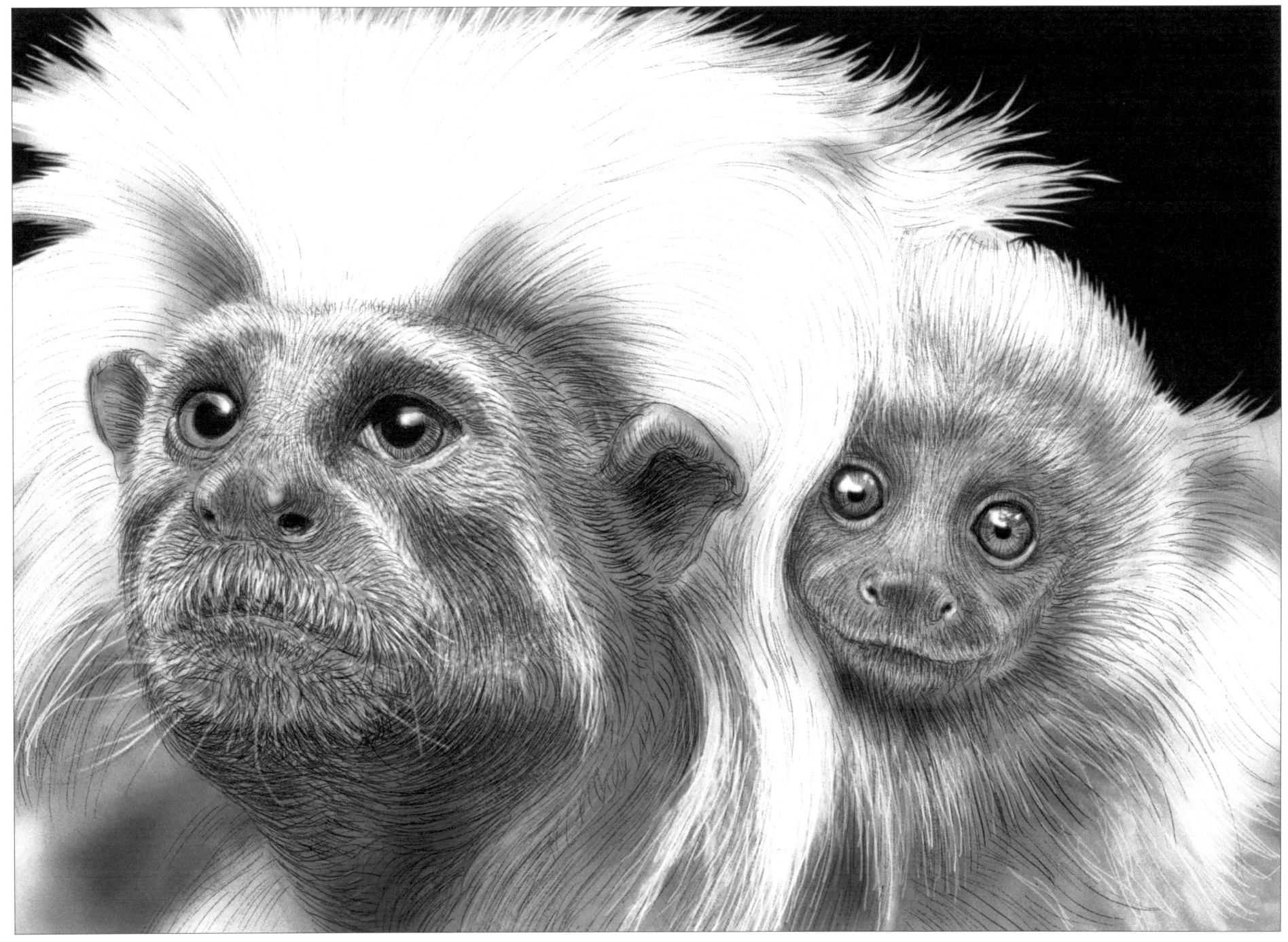

Cotton-Top Tamarins

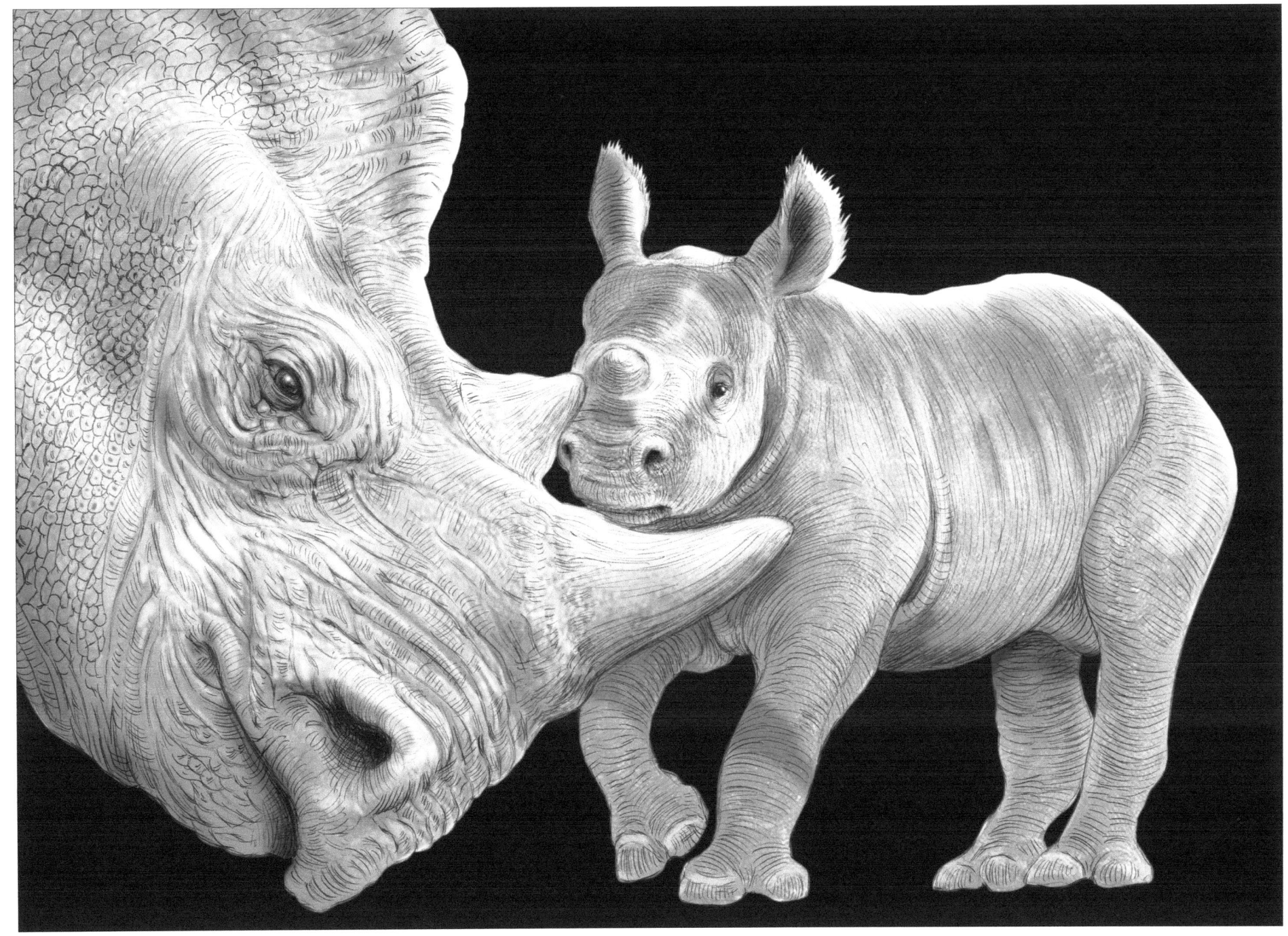

Eastern Black Rhinoceros

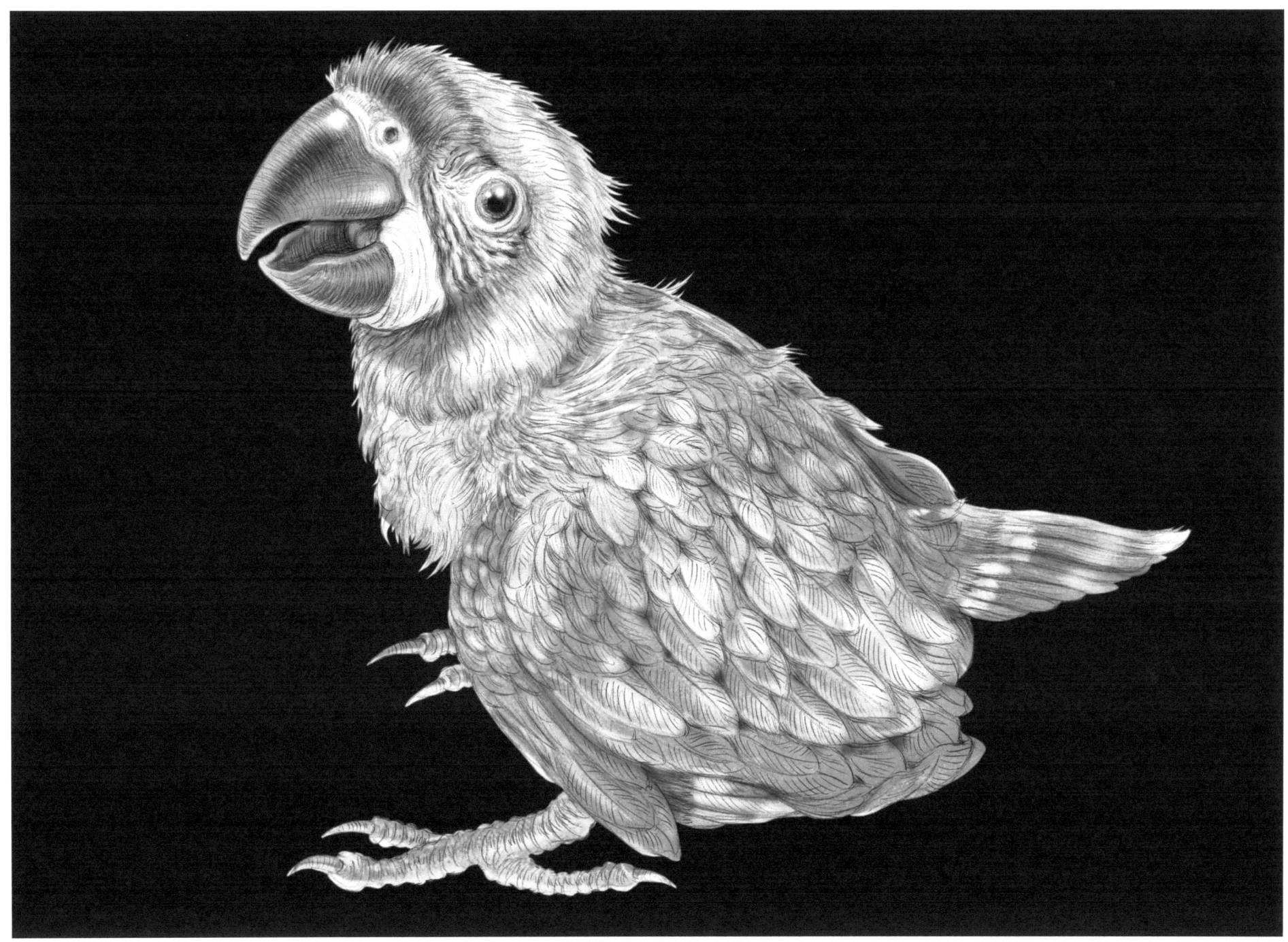

Great Green Macaw

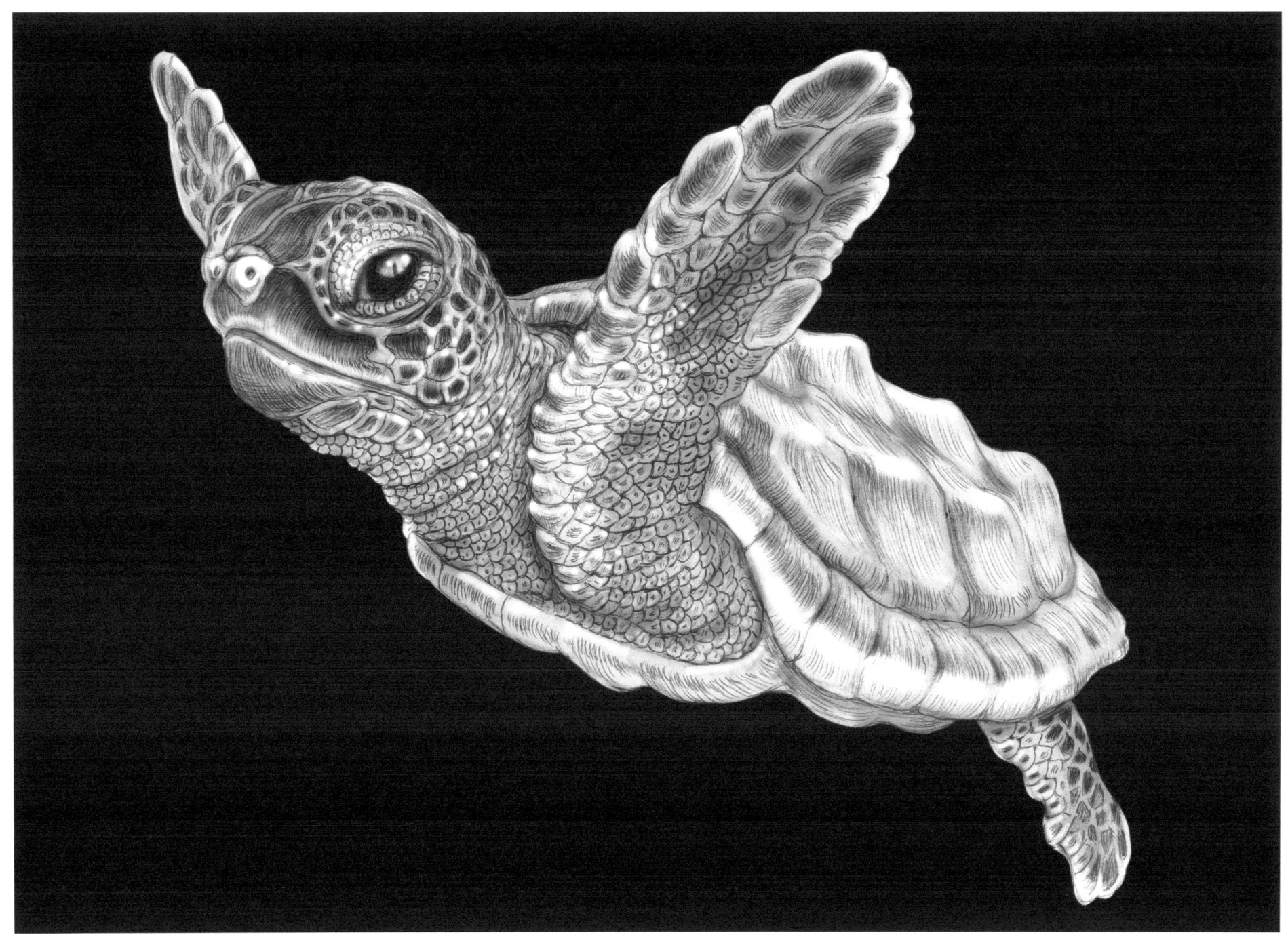

Hawksbill Sea Turtle

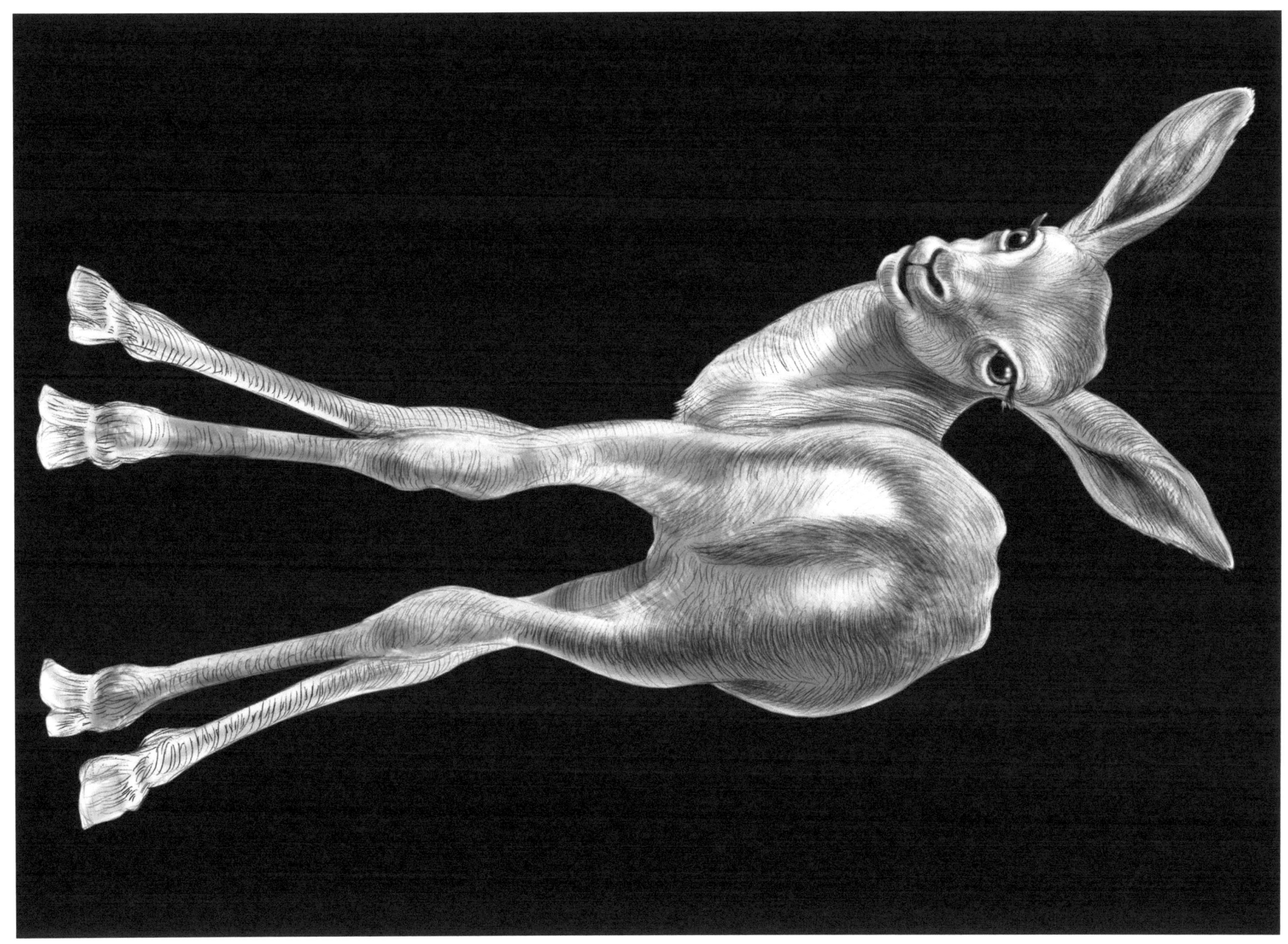

Mhorr Gazelle

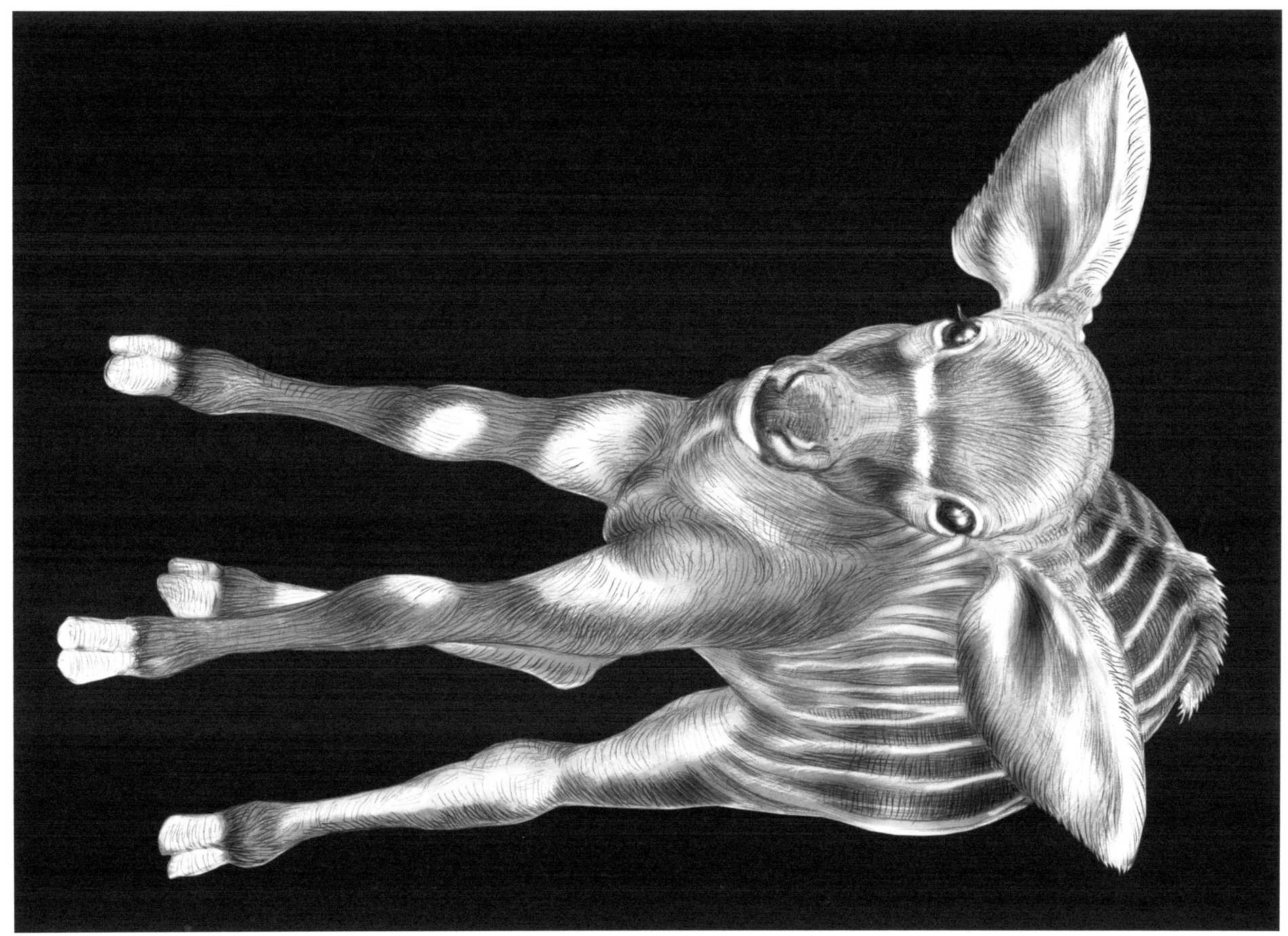

Mountain Bongo

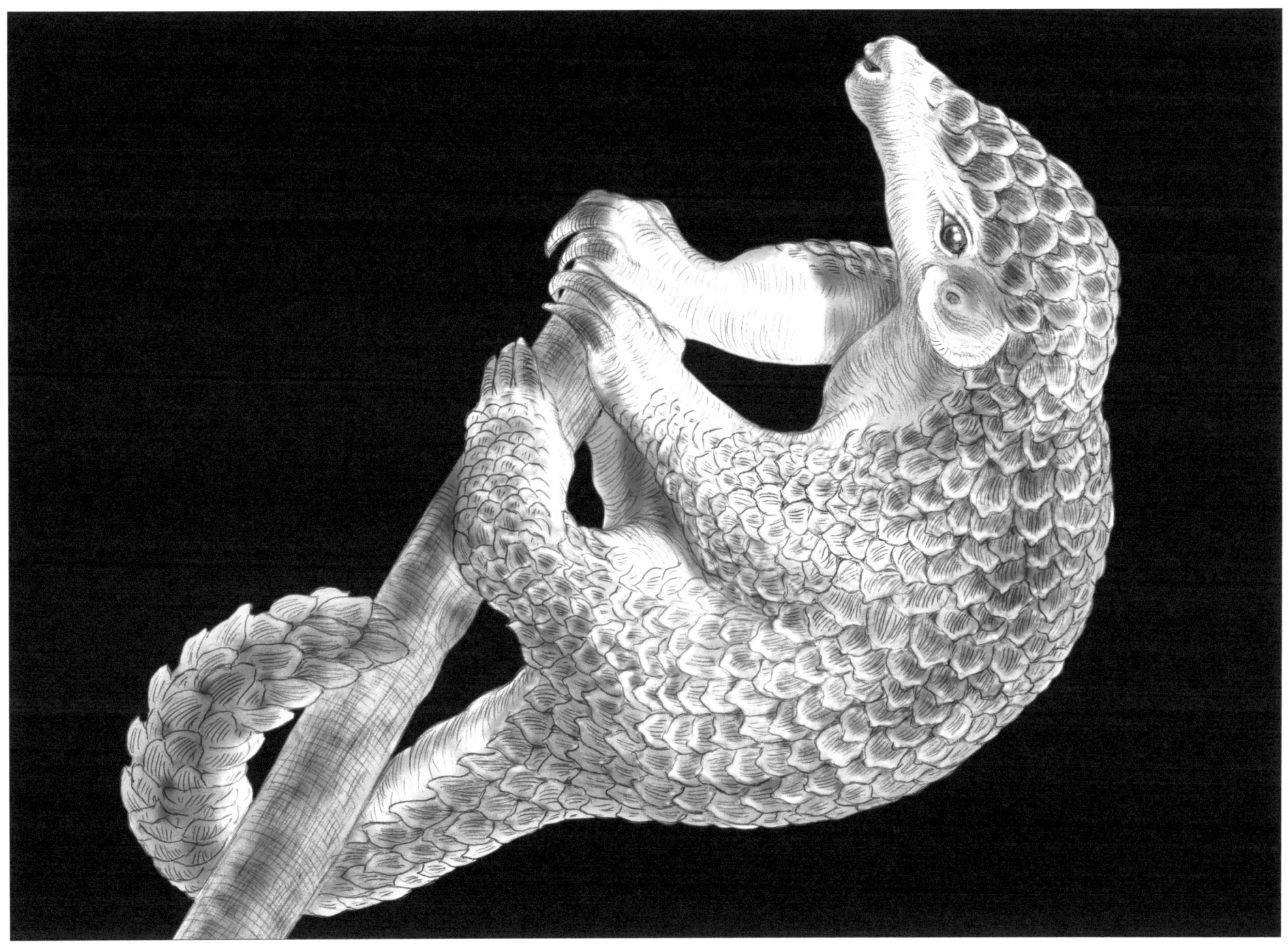

Pangolin

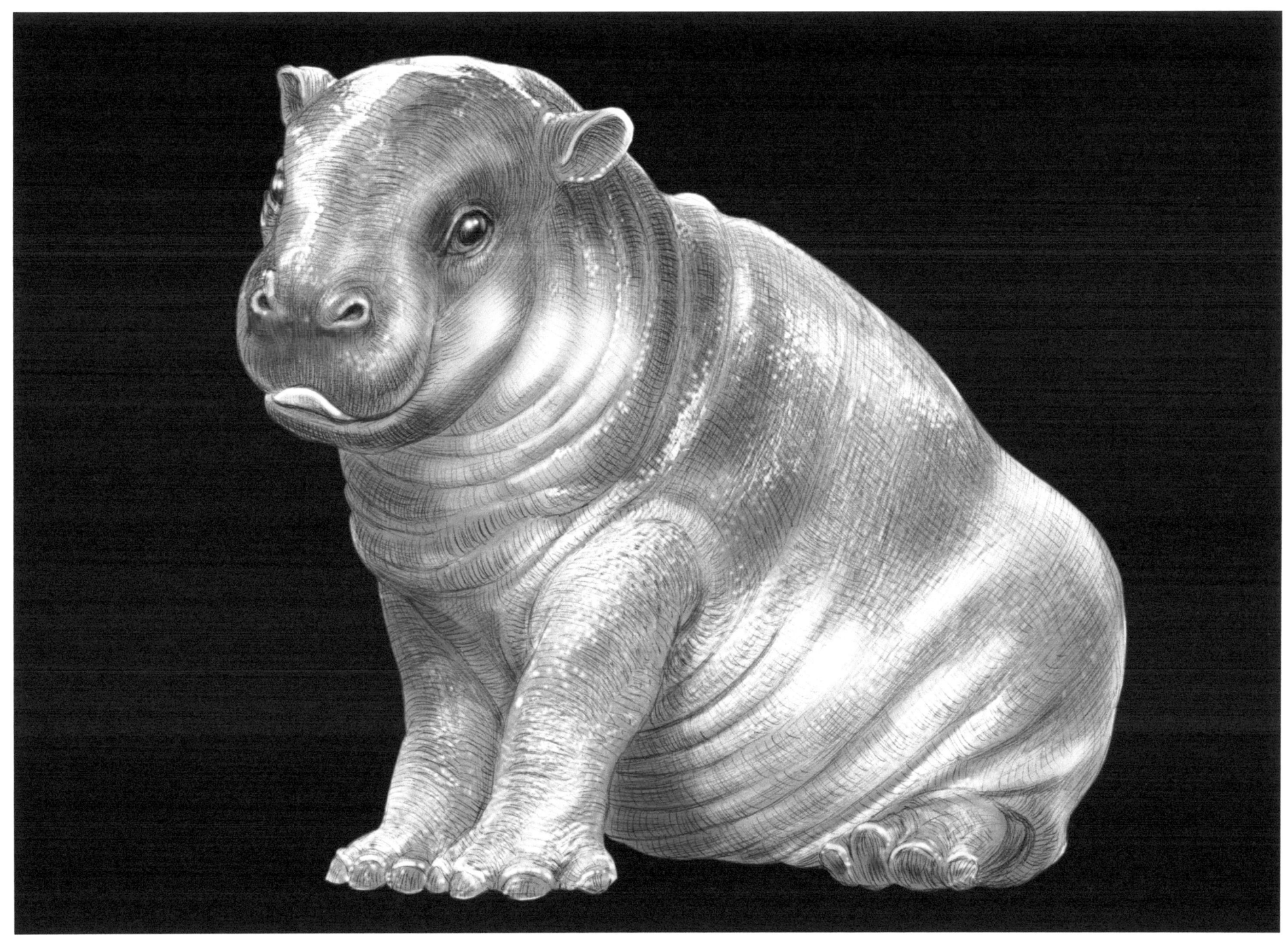
Pygmy Hippopotamus

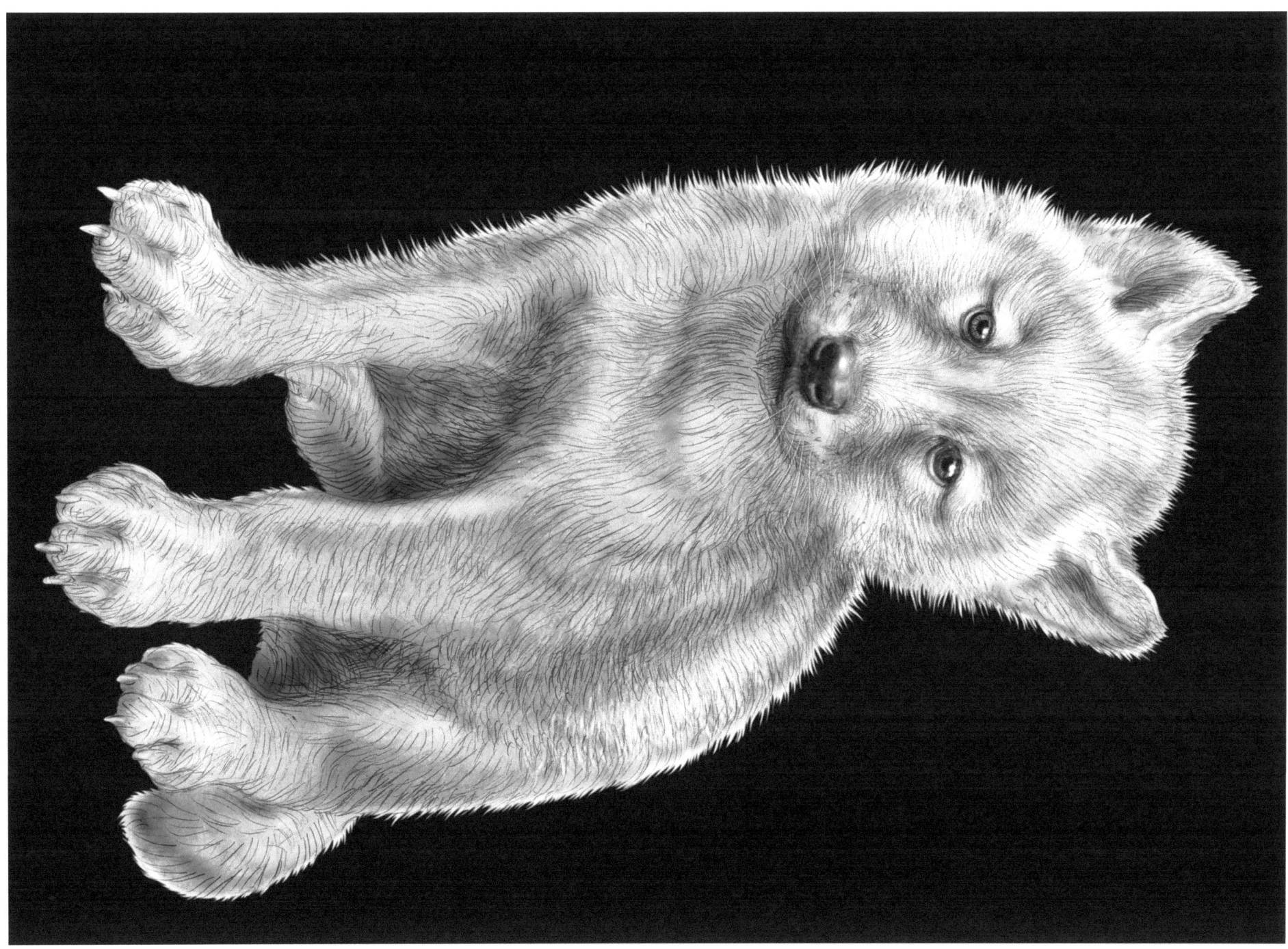

Red Wolf

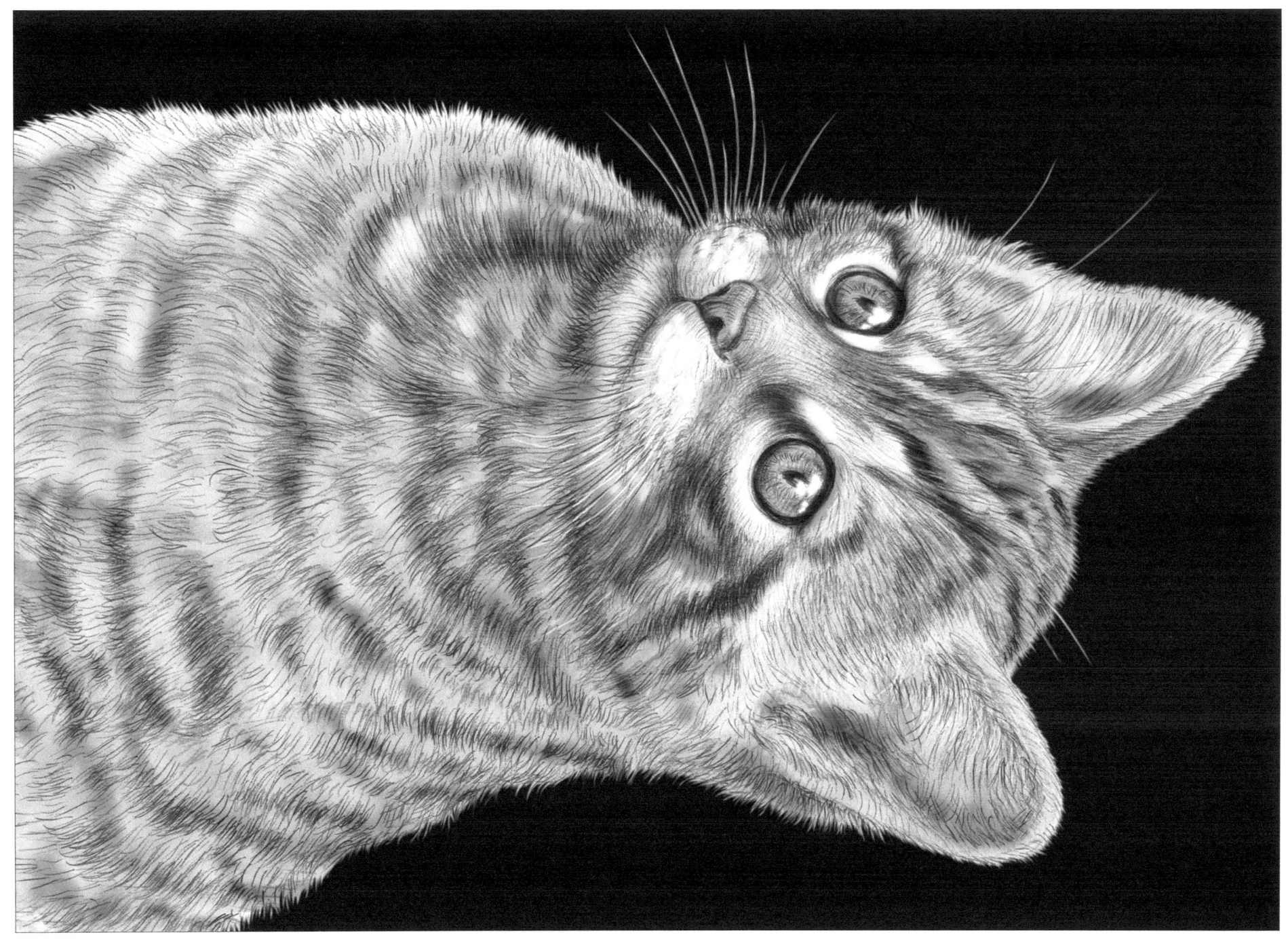

Scottish Wildcat

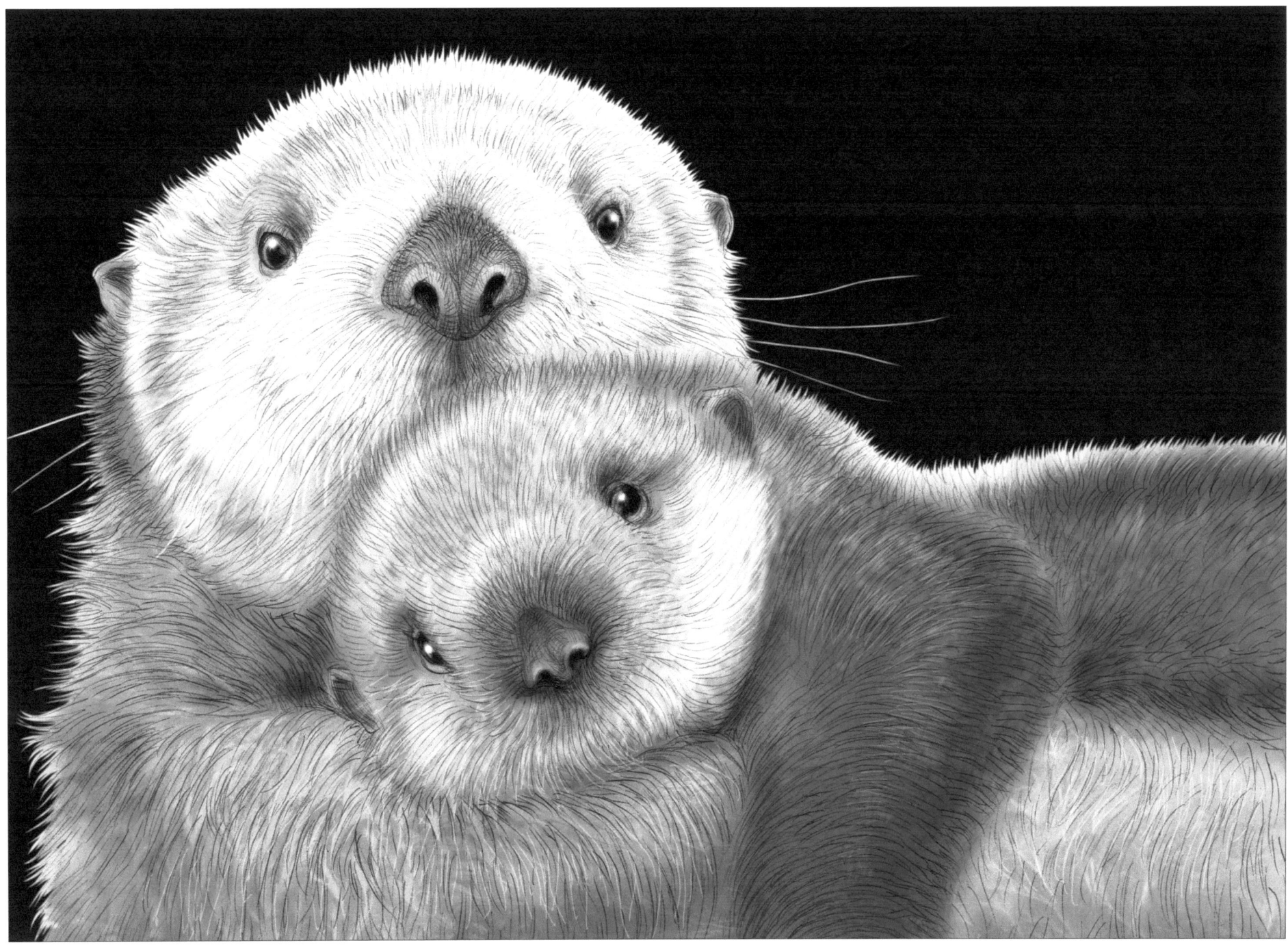

Sea Otters

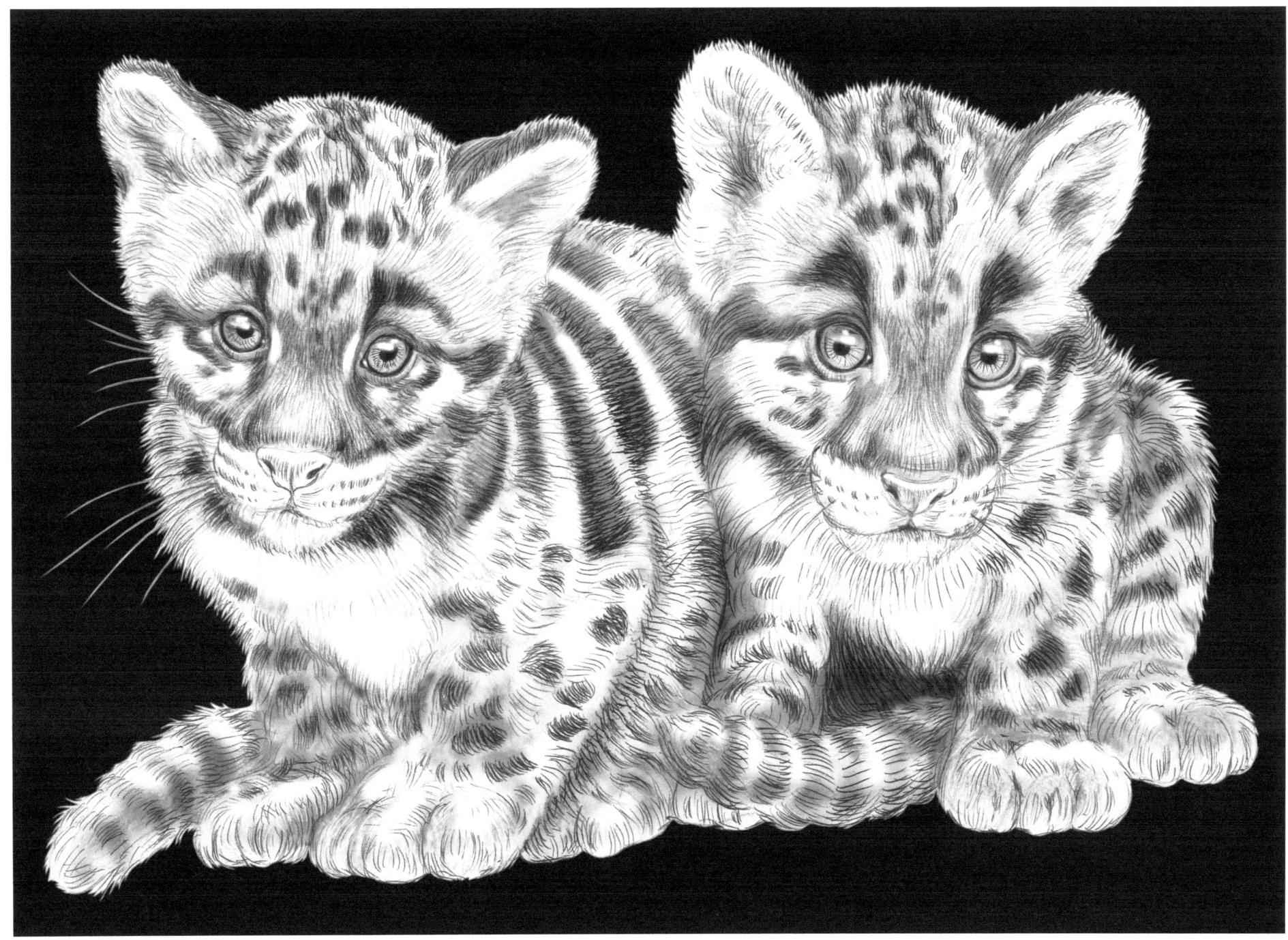

Snow Leopards

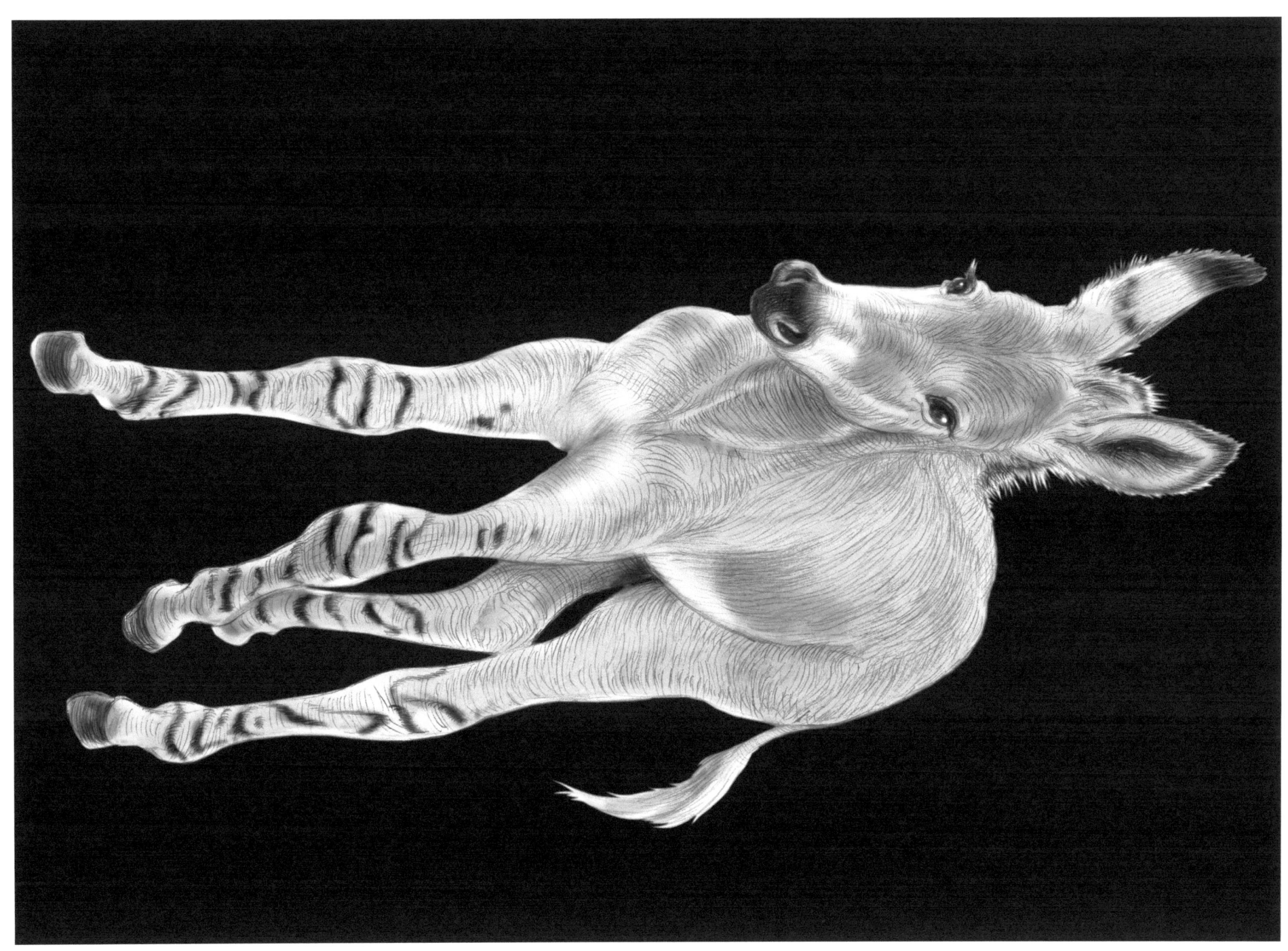

Somalia Wild Ass

Tim Jeffs is a New York City based artist and illustrator who has been creating dynamic artwork for over 25 years. Animals are a favorite subject matter of his, along with the complex and intricate details these creatures possess. *"The incredible diversity and complexity of animals has always intrigued me. They offer endless pleasure to look and marvel upon. In every drawing I try to capture the unique quality of each particular animal. I hope you enjoy my perspective, love and admiration of these incredible creatures."*

Visit my website for prints, digital coloring books and coloring lessons:

www.TimJeffsArt.com

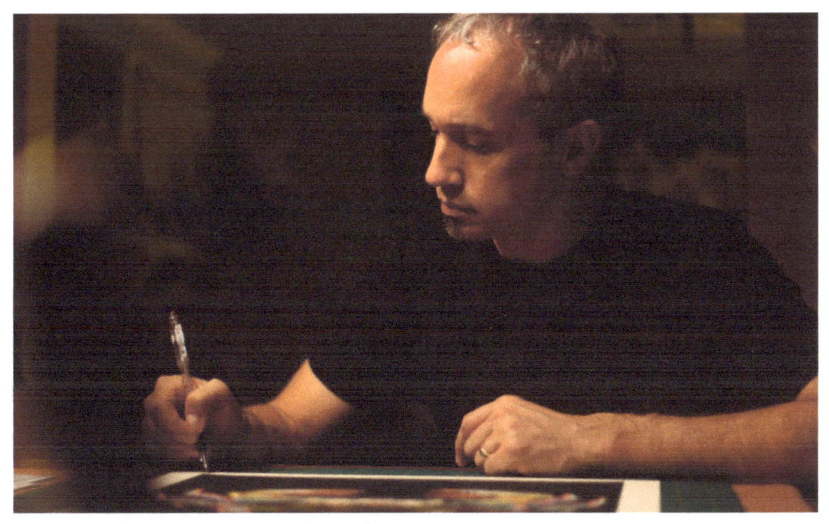

Discover the full line of Tim Jeffs' Published Coloring Books

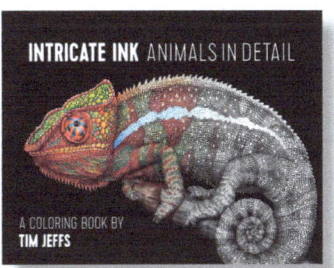 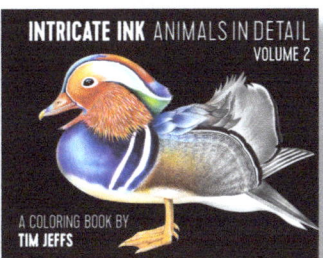 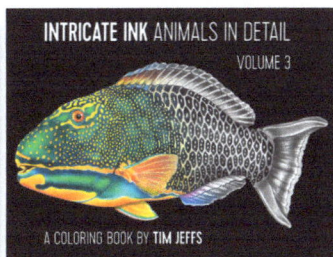 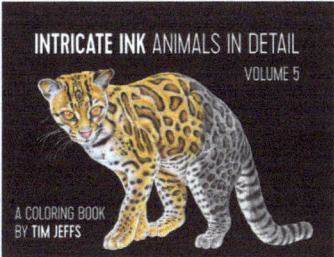 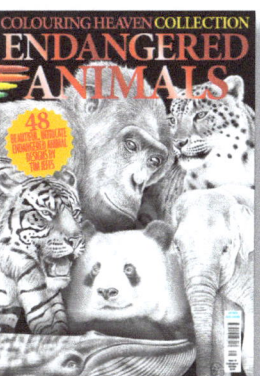

Intricate Ink Animals In Detail Volume 1, 2 3 and 5, and Intricate Animal Drawings Volume 1 and 2 are available at:
Amazon.com
Bookdepository.com

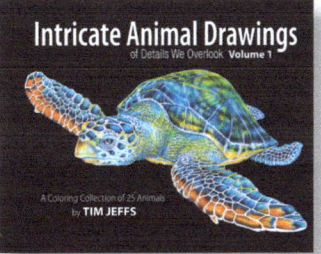 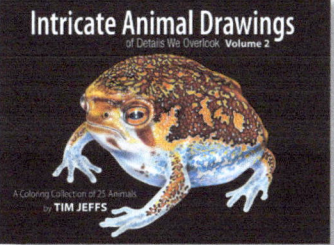

Colouring Heaven Collection Endangered Animals
Available at: Colouringheaven.com

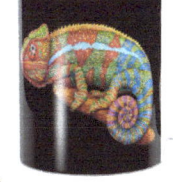

Discover Tim Jeffs' Merchandise

Etsy Shop
www.etsy.com/shop/TimJeffsArt

Society6 Shop
www.society6.com/TimJeffsArt

Redbubble Shop
TimJeffsArt.redbubble.com

TeePublic Shop
https://www.teepublic.com/user/tim-jeffs-art

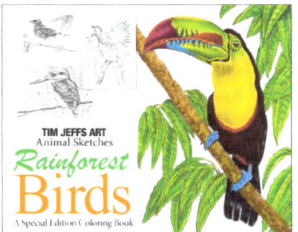

Discover the full line of Tim Jeffs Coloring Books and Lessons at
TimJeffsArt.com • Etsy.com • Amazon.com

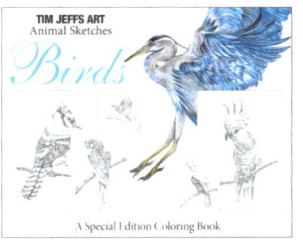 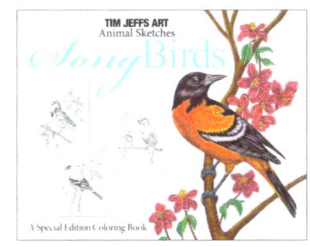
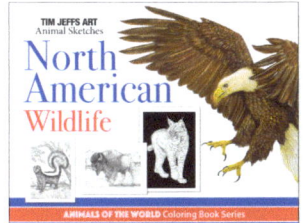 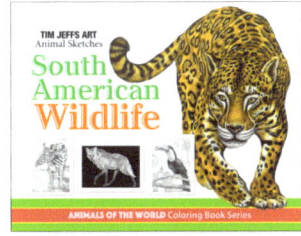 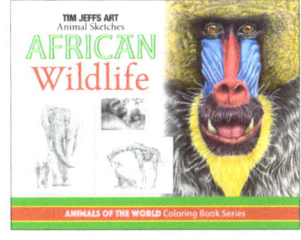 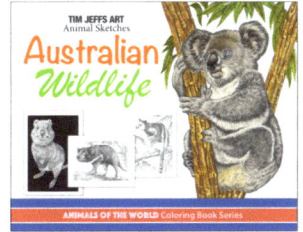 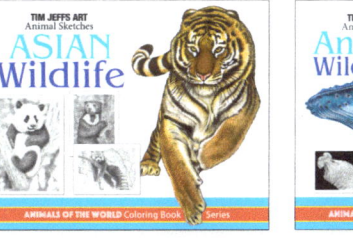 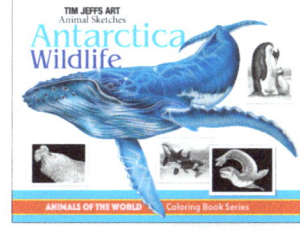
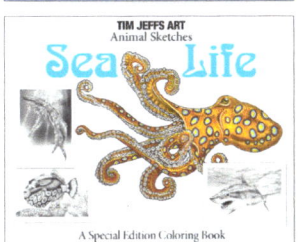 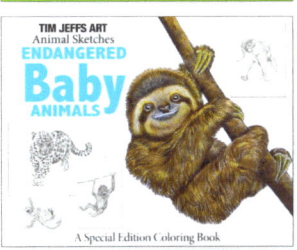 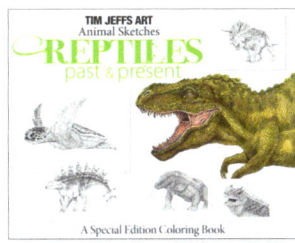 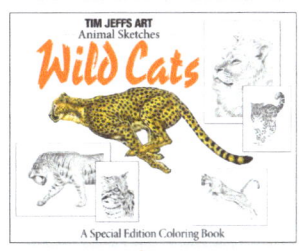 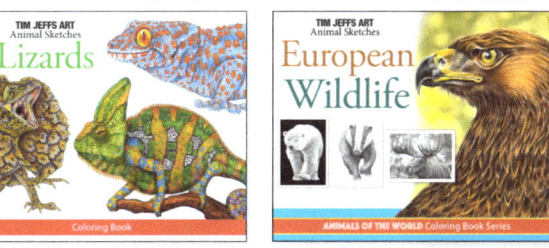
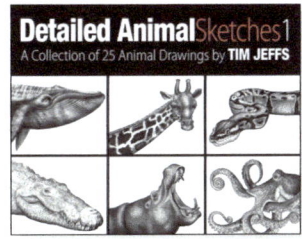 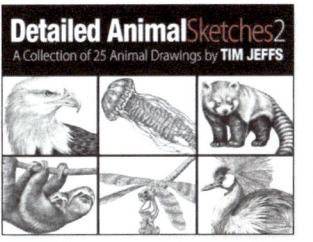 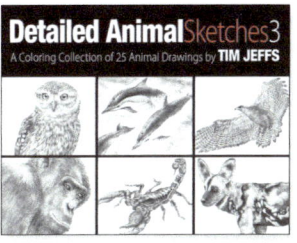 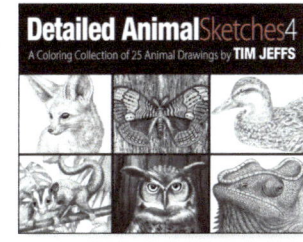 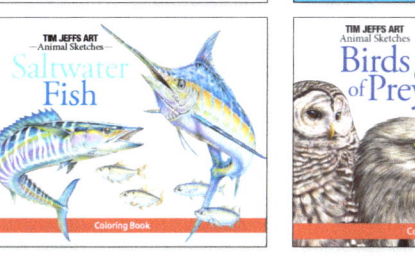 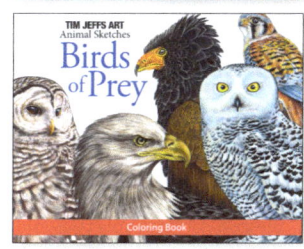
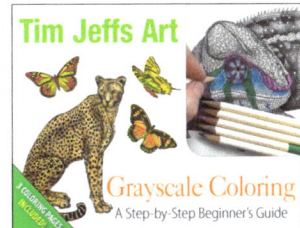 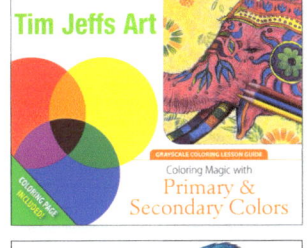 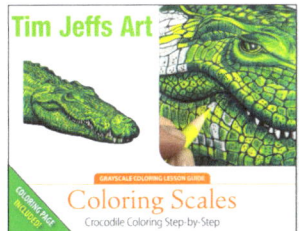 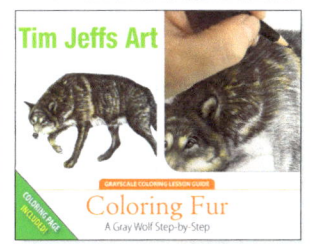 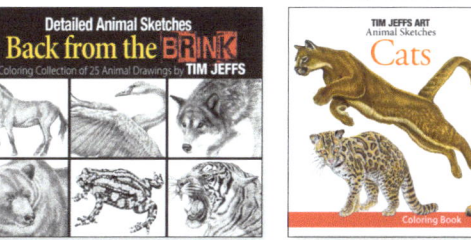
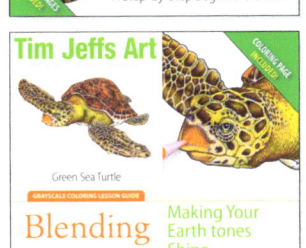 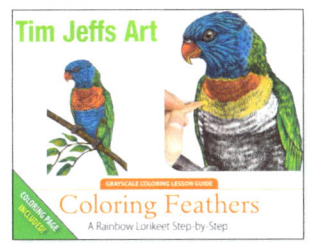 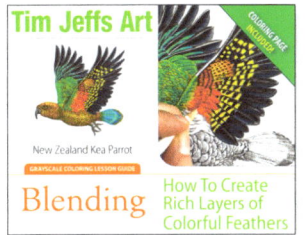 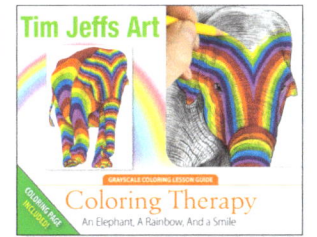 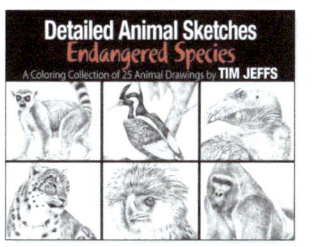 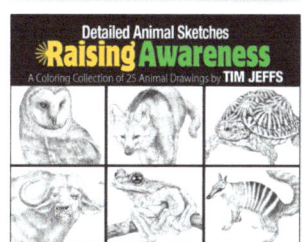

TIM JEFFS ART Online Resources

Share Your Creativity with the World!

Join the ever-expanding coloring group of animal lovers who inspire each other through their colorings of the animals from Tim's books and lessons. With thousands of members from all around the world, Tim's Facebook group "Intricate Ink Coloring Group" is a creative and safe space where everyone is welcome. Jo Warren, the groups all-inspiring administrator will welcome you in with open arms and is there to encourage everyone to just have fun no matter your coloring skill level. Come join, we can't wait to have you as a member! Join Tim's Facebook Coloring Group at:

www.facebook.com/groups/intricateink

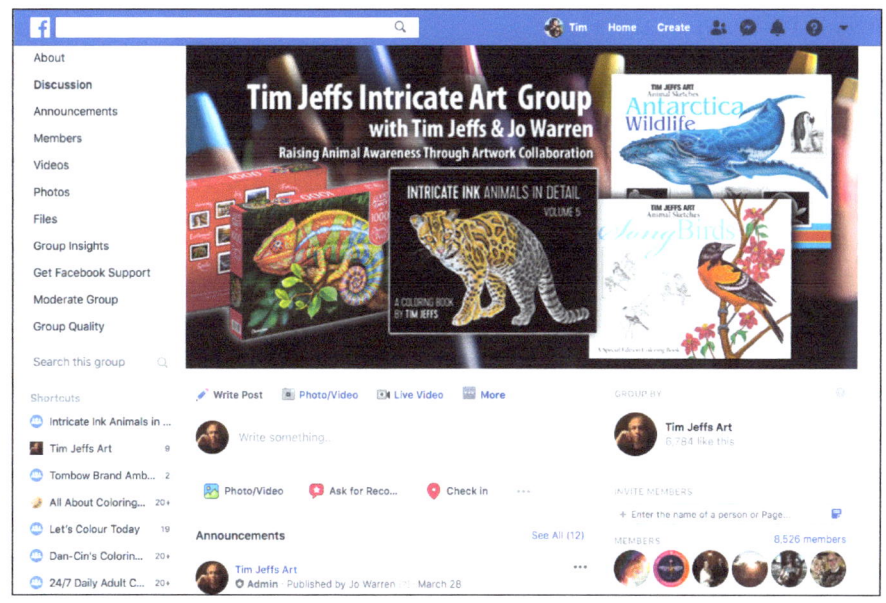

Visit the Home of Tim Jeffs Art

TimJeffsArt.com is my home on the web where I display all of my work and various projects. I hope you can stop by for a visit! You'll find my new shop where signed and unsigned prints of all of my animal drawings are available to purchase, along with the complete library of my digital download coloring books and grayscale coloring lessons. In the conservation section, you can see the projects that I am very proud of. Using my art to preserve wildlife is so important to me.

www.TimJeffsArt.com

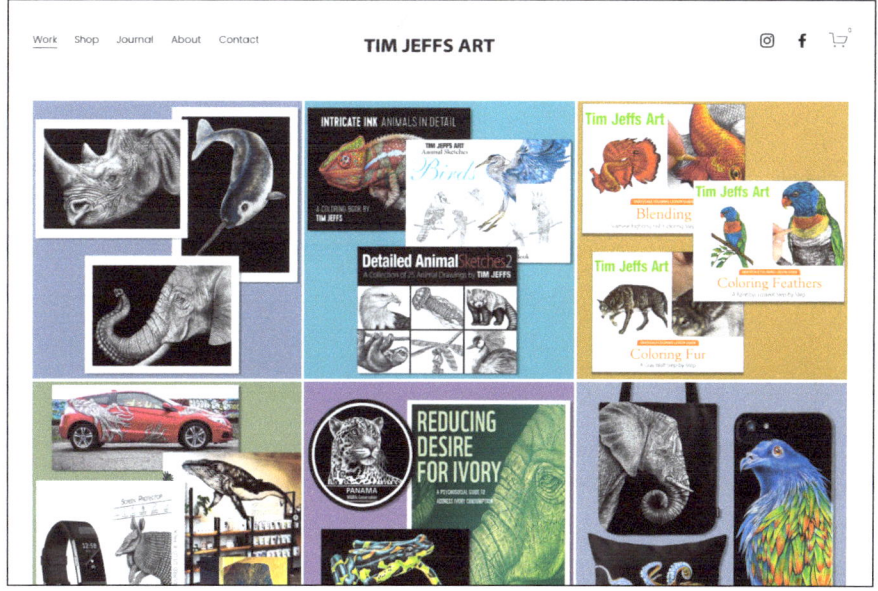